GOD GIVEN – GOD INSPIRED

PRODUCTIONS MADE PERSONAL

PMP – VOLUME 1

CREATED BY:

LUTHER T. COLLINS

Printed in the United States of America
Kingdom Minded Enterprises (Atlanta, GA)

© Copyright 2020 by Luther T. Collins

All rights reserved. This book or parts thereof may not be reproduced in any form, stored in a retrieval system, or transmitted in any form by any means-electronic, mechanical, photocopy, recording, or otherwise-without prior written permission of the author, except as provided by United States of America copyright law.

All Music, All Poetry, All Spoken Word
Written & Created by Luther T. Collins.
Cover Design by Javeria Saleem

ISBN: 978-1-7351253-2-9

To contact author for booking or ordering additional copies, go to:
luthertcollins0408@gmail.com

PMP – VOLUME 1

PRODUCTIONS READILY MADE BROUGHT TO YOU IN YOUR VERY OWN HOME DURING QUARANTINE TIME!

LAUGHTER IN YOUR VERY OWN LIVING ROOM!

ENTERTAINMENT FOR YOUR VERY OWN ENJOYMENT!

GOOD STORY ALL FOR GOD'S GLORY!

CLEAN COMEDY FOR ALL CONDITIONS!

FUN FOR ALL FAMILY MEMBERS!

REALITY IN REAL LIFE PRODUCTIONS!

GOD GIVEN – GOD INSPIRED

PRODUCTIONS MADE PERSONAL

PMP Contents

Production 1…..……What Would Jesus Do

Production 2………………..The Best In Me

Production 3…..When Purpose Meets Praise

Production 4…….Don't Change The Station

Production 5…….Together We Stand Part 1

God Given – God Inspired

Productions Made Personal

What Would Jesus Do

THROUGH GOD ALL THINGS ARE POSSIBLE!

Written & Produced By:

Brother Luther T. Collins

First Official Performance:

June 12, 2009 @ 7:30 pm

Introduction

This play was written to inspire young adults that we have to get off of our own agenda and get on Gods agenda. So many times in life we get so caught up that we leave God out of the equation. We tend to use God as a spare tire and only pull him out when we get in trouble. We take Gods goodness and mercy for granted. God is love, but his love for us won't override his word. Stop the judgment that one day determines our eternal resting place. It's time to take a stand and divorce the world today. Let go and let God lead you. Repent and turn from your evil ways before it's too late. Before you make any decisions in life ask yourself, What Would Jesus Do?

Main Characters

Roles	Titles
Minister Innis **Brother Louis**	**Musician**
Pastor Palby Latté Ramón **Brother Luther**	**Pastor**
Evangelist Kizzi Ramón **Sister Tasha**	**First Lady**
Tyree Jones **Brother Frank**	**Drug Dealer**
Brother Malcolm Fleas **Brother Frank**	**Drummer**
Sister Umba Cotae **Sister Shelia**	**Usher**
Sister Camelle Collins **Sister Kristina**	**Choir Member**
Sister Renita Spinks **Sister Alfreda**	**Choir Member**

Deputy Dean Lonabar **Brother Rashad**	**Sheriff**
Junior Hamlett **Brother Rashad**	**Keyboardist**
Sister Shevell Chevorlett **Sister Ketara**	**Choir Member**

Scene 1

Junior Hamlett: (Dims lights in the front as everyone takes there places)

Music Minister directs choir singing "The Presence of the Lord" by Byron Cage

Heartfelt and very passionate song ministry for the gospel until the Pastor begins to sing

Messing up the song (All off note and very loud)

Minister Innis: HOLD UP! STOP THE MUSIC! Hold Up Me Say! Stop The Music Right Now!

Junior Hamlett: (Stops music while laughing aloud and pointing at Pastor)

Minister Innis: Pastor Palby Latté Ramón, What's up? You Messing Up My Song!

Pastor Palby: I Just, I Just, I Just feel his presence! Hallelujah! I just got to sing and praise as good as God has been to me.

Minister Innis: Correct me if I'm wrong but doesn't it say, make a joyful noise? No disrespect Pastor Ray Ray but nothing about your singing says joyful! Hallelujah!

Brother Malcolm: (Looking at Minister Innis) Minister Innis you know Pastor just can't hold a note! It's not his fault it's in his blood!

Minister Innis: Bless his heart! Brother Malcolm Fleas, can I get a microphone check? And can somebody please turn Pastors mic down, LOW!

Pastor Palby: Praise the lord saints as I try to contain myself.

Minister Innis: Okay let's take it from the top! "I can feel the Presence of the Lord" (Directing the choir as they sing and dance out of control in harmony)

Sister Umba Cotae: (Stands up passes her bible to the person sitting beside her) Hold this for me for a second (And starts shaking)

Pastor Palby: Praise the Lord Sister Umba Cotae

Sister Umba Cotae: Praise the Lord Pastor (Falling out under the power still shaking)

Minister Innis: (Closes out the song)

Pastor Palby: Praise the Lord Saints! (Everyone looking around and carrying on in the choir and pulpit) I said Praise the Lord Saints (With a loud and aggressive voice)! For this is the day that the lord has made and we shall rejoice and be glad in it! Minister Innis won't you come up and give us this morning's announcements.

Minister Innis: (Goes up to the podium shaking and shouting still carrying on in the spirit in praise) Praise the Lord Saints! Welcome to Saints of the Sanctuary Presbyterian Baptismal Episcopal Cath-letic Church. And I just want to say to all of you this morning, I can feel the Presence of Lord …….. (Singing as the choir and Pastor stands to join in)

(Brings song to a close) Now back to our regularly scheduled announcements!

Minister Innis: (Pauses for a minute while tapping his feet and hitting his hand against his leg) Excuse me for a minute while I get my church on

Pastor Palby: (Walks over to the keyboard and starts to play off key)

Brother Malcolm: GREAT DAY! Do we have any keyboard players in the house?

Junior Hamlett: (Takes over the keyboard and pushes Pastor out the way)

Minister Innis: (Dances down the aisle losing his wig in the process until he falls out)

Pastor Palby: (Catches him)

Minister Innis: (Flips himself up continuing to praise as he grabs Sister Cheverolett to join him in praise until they fall out together after doing the kid and play with no movement)

Pastor Palby: That concludes this morning's announcements

End of Scene 1

Scene 2

Pastor Palby: (Begins to go into his sermon)

Today church we are going to talk about, "What Would Jesus Do?" You know you have to get to a point where we ask ourselves, what would Jesus do when we fall short and get to that state of weakness.

Sister Umba Cotae: (Snoring loud in the back)

Pastor Palby: You betta wake up Sister Umba Coate before I throw this good book and bust you upside your head with the love of the lord! You hear me now!

Sister Umba Cotae: Oh I'm sorry Pastor I was daydreaming about some chitlin stir fry

(Goes on about chitlins and leads the choir in chitlin celebration)

Pastor Palby: That's okay sister I forgive you now let's just get back to this word.

Like I was saying you have to ask yourself what would Jesus do. Since yall looking at me all crazy, let me, let me break it down in rich dummy terms for you all. When you are in the club shaking it fast you have to ask yourself (Points to the congregation for response), When you're in line for that payday loan and they deny you because you don't have a job you have to ask yourself (Points to the congregation for response), When your husband acting like a fool you have to ask yourself (Points to the congregation for response), When your wife acting like a fool you have to ask yourself (Points to the congregation for response), When your children out there imitating Lil Wizzil, 30 Cent, and Jay C you have to ask yourself (Points to the congregation for response), When your running low on life and Dionne Warwick won't give you any more advice you have to ask yourself (Points to the congregation for response), When your food stamp card has been revoked you have to ask yourself (Points to the congregation for response), When you have to take your yackey to the pond shop and trade it in for a Beverly Johnson you have to ask yourself (Points to the congregation for response), When you go to the car dealership and have to trade in your 76 Cutlass Supreme for a 36 BC Pinto Bean you have to ask yourself (Points to the congregation for response)!

Evangelist Kizzi: 36 BC

Choir Members: (Looking at each other says together) 36 BC

Sister Umba Cotae: (Stands up looking confused while straightening her wig) 36 BC

Pastor Palby: Yeah before Christ and I ain't talking about Chrysler!

See you as the believer have to ask yourself, What Yo Daddy Doing?

Evangelist Kizzi: (Stands up with a loud voice) My daddy in heaven tap dancing on the devil's head! Amen Pastor!

Pastor Palby: Amen Evangelist Kizzi Sisilla Ramón, my beautiful, awesome, obedient, anointed, loving, blessed and highly favored woman of God! As a matter of fact I got something for you…. (Pauses and begins to sing You Are So Beautiful To Me)

(Interrupted by loud noise and someone running in the church with a lot of commotion)

Tyree: (Does a tuck and roll entering into the church, runs around the church through the aisles and in between people and runs back to the door to peep out the door while ducking as he's on the run from the police)

Minister Innis: (Stands Up) Praise the Lord for another lost soul in the house!

Tyree: You talking about me boy! (Takes Minister Innis's wig off and puts it in his chest) I isn't lost I'm just on the run from the Po Pos

Minister Innis: (Looking around to see who he's talking to) The Devil is a Liar! Hallelujah! (Raises his hands in praise)

Sheriff Dean Lonabar: Comes in flashing his badge and gun asking if anyone seen an escaped convict in the area?

Tyree: (Points his gun at Minister Innis)

Minister Innis: No Deputy Lonabar we haven't seen no crazy folks around here not as long as they packing pieces and I ain't talking bout Reeses.

Sheriff Dean Lonabar: Well if there's no danger than my work here is done! (Walking out) But I'll be back!

Tyree: (Starts walking around and looking over people when the pastor beings to preach again)

Pastor Ramón: (Preaches over the commotion) the question remains what would Jesus do? Now turn with me if you will to Philippians 2:21 (KJV) and say Amen when you get there (Pastor reads the scripture). So based on this when you seek the world you get results of the world. For God said anyone who chooses to follow him will be blessed and receive eternal life. I don't know about you but nothing on this earth is worth going to hell for.

Tyree: (Walks over to a member) would you like to buy a bag of seeds lady?

Minister Innis: Are they do-good seeds?

Tyree: (Looks around) I got green trees, blue trees, sunflower seeds, white powder cake, shake and bake, now laters, and alligators! So which will it be? Hugh?

Tyree: (Responds based on reaction from audience)

Minister Innis: (Stands up) I don't believe you have the audacity to come up in The Saints of The Sanctuary Presbyterian Baptismal Episcopal Cathletic Church with your isms and schisms trying to make a dollar out of 15 cent to pay your child support, lights, electric, and rent!

All Choir Members: Yea, You need to leave now!

Pastor Palby: What would Jesus do?

Tyree: I don't know! You tell me cause I'm just trying to get my paper. Can you feel me?

Sheriff Dean Lonabar: (Walks in adjusting his pants and sits in the back as he observes the convict while radioing in to his fellow police officers)

Pastor Palby: (Flips open his bible to a certain page) Jesus would say love conquerors a multitude of things. I love you even when you sold those non prescription drugs. I have a special assignment for your life. You have to divorce the world to fulfill this divine destiny that's been assigned to your life. Repent from your evil ways first and then go and sin no more.

Tyree: (Screams Out) But I don't want this life anymore! Yall just don't understand what it's like running from cops, ducking and dodging bullets daily, disgracing my mom, losing friends, being subject to peer pressure, drinking and drugging! Nobody understands! Please just take it away from me!

Pastor Palby: It's alright son! Jesus says receive him now and your sins will be remembered no more.

Tyree: Tell me what to do Pastor and I'll do it!

Pastor Ramón: Come down to the altar, drop the drugs and weapons at the altar, and just repeat after me. Let me get everyone to stretch their hands towards this young man.

Sheriff Dean Lonabar: (Walks to the altar and begins putting the drugs and money in his pocket)

Sister Umba Cotae: (Goes to the altar and lays hands on the sheriff while singing in tongue and he falls out under the power)

Choir Members: (Circle around the altar praise dancing over Tyree and Deputy)

Evangelist Kizzi: (Walks over and sprinkles salt and pepper over their heads)

Deputy Lonabar: I'm just so lonely! Help Me! Help Me Please!

Pastor Palby: You're in the right place Deputy now everyone stretch your hands towards them and repeat after me. Father you are the Christ, Son of the living God, I believe you died for me, set me free, forgive me for all my sins. I've done wrong but right now I change loyal ships. I make Jesus Christ Lord and Savior of my life therefore I am saved. Use me for your kingdom in a mighty way!

Praise the Lord Sons! You just made the most important decision of your life. Will there be anymore? (Pauses) Well since everyone's saved let's give God a hand clap of praise for his goodness and mercy while the napkin is still folded.

Since all minds are clear Minister Innis is going to close us out in song (Signals for Minister Innis to come up and lead the church out with the closing song)

Minister Innis: (Leads in song What Would Jesus Do)

What Would Jesus Do

Though times are tough

And the mountains seem so rough

Getting hard to hold on

To everything you know is true

If you just believe

God will pull you through

For God sees everything

Everything you do and don't do

If you just call on his name

In the mist of the storm

He'll restore your light

No matter how dark it is at night

Can you somebody tell me

Can you tell me?

What would Jesus Do?

Pastor Palby: (Concluding the Song) The doors of the church are open saints!

The End

The Best In Me

Written & Produced By:

Brother Luther T. Collins

Introduction

    Not everyone you meet or come in contact during the course of your life will see the best in you. In fact it seems as if you meet more people when you're going through tough times in your life. People can only be people as we cannot expect anything more. The key to going through is not letting it show on the outside as it's a lot easier said than done. Never let rainy days wash away your sunshine as joy comes in the morning.

Characters

Sharlice Biggs   Mother
Sister Danita

Tiny Biggs   Father
Brother Luther

Unique Biggs   Daughter
Sister Aniyah

Evernesia   Grandma
Sister Mary

Cleophsis   Grandpa
Deacon Keith

Scene 1:

(Music Playing "He Saw The Best In Me" by Marvin Sapp)

Sharlice: (Cleaning house while mimicking song with mop handle)

Tiny: (Walks in the house with his nappy afro wearing his old hand me down 70's threads slamming the door behind him) Turn down that music Sharlice. You know better than to have that music blasting like that. And who all these people in my house?

Sharlice: (Turns down radio) All those people are the audience silly. And last time I checked my daddy name was Cleophisis Samone Sugarbear.

Tiny: Yeah whatever! I wouldn't tell nobody that though they might think you got the cooties or something.

Sharlice: Well at least his momma didn't name him something that would stunt his growth. Know what I mean Tiny Toonbox Biggs!

Tiny: Oh, you wanna go there hugh! How do you explain yo mamma name? Evernesia! I guess that's why she always says you can call me if you ever needs a.

Sharlice: (Turns radio back up)

Tiny: (Walks over and cuts radio off)

Sharlice: Boy you got some nerve! (Pauses as Unique walks in the room)

Unique: Hi daddy (Gives dad a hug), how was your day today

Tiny: Let's see I lost my job, had my car stolen, and lost my lunch money but other than that everything was cool

Sharlice: You did what!

Tiny: You heard me I said I lost my job!

Sharlice: How did you lose your job Tiny?

Tiny: My boss said I was flirting with his wife?

Unique: What does flirting mean daddy?

Sharlice: Go to your room baby

Unique: Man I never get to see the good stuff (Walks out to her room)

Sharlice: What did you say to Mr. Bedrock's wife

Tiny: All I said was she looks beautiful today

Sharlice: (Pops Tiny in the back of the head) Un hugh

Tiny: And if Mr. Bedrock can't keep up to give me a call for a follow up inspection

Sharlice: You said what? Naw never mind that how did my car get stolen?

Tiny: I went to get me a 40 ounce of mad dog on my lunch break cause I was thirsty and somebody drove off with the car while I was in the store on the North Side

Sharlice: So basically you left my car running unattended while you were in the store buying beer

Tiny: I was watching it from the inside

Sharlice: You know what it's time for you to go

Tiny: Say what, say hugh, say who, say how you gone do that

Sharlice: Get yo stuff and get the steppin that's how (Giving demonstration)

Tiny: Fool you must be crazy I paid the rent 2 months ago and I even cut the grass and washed your junky car last month.

Sharlice: I don't know who you think you talking to. If I'm a fool than yo mama a fool. You the man of the house I hope you would carry your fair share of the workload.

Tiny: If it wasn't for your spending habits than maybe we could have something decent in this house to show for.

Unique: (Comes out of her room) Is everything okay mom and dad?

Sharlice: Yes baby, your daddy was just leaving

Tiny: I ain't going nowhere. I got rights you know! We in the land of the free, home of the slave I mean brave and I say I'm staying.

Sharlice: Over my dead body negro.

Unique: Can't yall two just get along.

Tiny: Sorry you had to hear this baby girl but yo mama just can't get herself together

Sharlice: Tiny Toonbox Biggs you are a sorry excuse for a man and I don't ever want to see your sorry but again!
(Sharlice walks out and slams door)

(Light dim)

End of Scene 1

Scene 2

(Sharlice is in her mother's room)

Evernesia: (Laying down in the bed and turns around) What is it baby? What's wrong (Gets up out the bed and sits down as she directs Sharlice to sit in a chair across from her)

Sharlice: Ma I just can't take it no more. Tiny has disrespected me for the last time. I don't trust him and I don't want to be with him no more. He lost his job and he lost my car. He's a sorry excuse for a man I say.

Evernesia: What do you mean he lost your car baby?

Sharlice: He went to that mom and pops store on the Northside to buy a 40 ounce of mad dog and left the car running for someone to steal.

Evernesia: First off Sharlice you got it all wrong. There is no 40 ounce of mad dog 20/20. I know this because me and your father used to fill our little sippy cups in our day and the bottle was never big enough for the both of us. He probably got a 40 ounce of the bull, Schlitz Malt Liquor that is! I may be saved sanctified and full of the Holy Ghost but I ain't always been this way. We have to go through the process first.

Sharlice: What process is that mama?

Evernesia: The process of life baby. You take yourself for instance. You remember how many times I had to come out school led alone how many but whippings you got for that mouth of yours?

Sharlice: But we not talking about me mama. This ain't about me.

Evernesia: That's where your wrong baby. God did not create perfect people, we all have faults and we have to learn to consider ourselves first. It's not for us to judge others but for us to get it together ourselves. How can you tell someone else what they're doing wrong if you're in the wrong yourself?

Sharlice: But ma, Tiny has lost his job, he half way pays bills, he barely cleans up after himself

Evernesia: Hold up now, let me stop you there. Do you hear yourself; there you go again worrying about him. What if I said Sharlice spends money faster than it comes in this house, Sharlice does not give compliments, Sharlice does not spend time with her family, Sharlice has a mouth on her! You see my point.

Sharlice: Yes ma but what do I do. I just don't have the patience to deal with this anymore.

Evernesia: Sure you do. It all starts with those words that you allow to come out of your mouth. Baby you have to speak life and learn to pray when test and trials come your way. Not every day is going to be shopping sprees and fairytale magazines.

Sharlice: Yes ma your right but.

Evernesia: No buts you have to let go and let God. When was the last time you prayed for your marriage?

Sharlice: Umm, Umm

Evernesia: My point exactly you have to give it to God. Be swift to hear and slow to speak my child. Stop pointing the blame and start praying for rain. If it doesn't work it's just as much your fault as his.

Sharlice: So what do I do ma to make things right?

Evernesia: Search your heart and find the best in him. It's so easy to see the faults and what he does wrong. But think back to when you first met and how he was able to steal your heart. You have to reignite the fire and restore the magic in your marriage. If you do this than you will build him up versus tear him down. You do your part and God will handle the rest.

Sharlice: I guess I could do a little more to help in my marriage.

Evernesia: I'd say. Poor Tiny had to sell his Play Station 3, basketball cards, and big screen television set just so you could have some shopping money. I never heard of so much foolishness in all my days. And child I've had many days!

Sharlice: I know mama. I think I got it now.

Evernesia: Don't take it for granted that you have a husband. My Pastor once said if you're not happy with your mate to buy your happiness because you can't change mates it's like changing your deodorant. It's just something you just don't do.

Sharlice: Say what?

Evernesia: If you don't like his smile get him a new set of dentures. If you're tired of his old spice get his some cool water cologne. If you don't like his tired ol leisure suits get him some tailor made Steve Harvey suits. If you don't like his Alvin & the Chipmunk Pajamas get him some Sean John PJ's. If you don't like his silver teeth buy him some gold fronts. If you don't like his Don King afro, give him some Snoop Doggy Dogg braids.

Sharlice: Okay mama I think I got your point. I need to dress my man up so when I see him well let's just say I see him. Sorry Lord, I guess it's a good thing only you could hear my thoughts.

(Baby girl walks in the room)

Unique: Hey mama & big mama, everything all right

Evernesia: Everything fine doll baby, just having some girl talk

Unique: Okay, let me know if you need anything

Sharlice: Actually we do baby, we were just about to say a prayer for our family and we were wondering if you would do us the honors.

Unique: You mean it! Sure!

Father God we thank you for the trees, the moons, the stars, the house, the clothes, the car oops that's gone, but we thank you Lord for the things we still have, our food, our family, our love, and may you restore our smiles on today. In Jesus name Amen!

End of Scene 2

Scene 3

Sharlice: (On her knees praying for God to restore her marriage) Oh God, forgive me for not being a good wife. Help me Lord not to find fault in others and give me strength to weather the storms that may come my way. Oh gracious God I honor you for who you are, you are worthy of all the honor, all the glory, and all the praise in Jesus name. Amen!

Cleophsis: (Standing over Sharlice as she prays) Oh child I forgive you.

Sharlice: Daddy what are you doing here, is that really you, you're supposed to be dead!

Cheophisis: Indeed but I just earned my wings today and I asked God if I could get a 15 minute break because that altar work will wear you down. Girl we been praying and pleading the blood over lost souls all day and all night!

Sharlice: Wait until I tell mama and everyone

Cleophisis: Only you can see me baby! They can't see me! I started to bring Matthew, Mark, Luke, & John but God's grace and mercy was running kind of low so I got out while I could.

Sharlice: Well how is it really in heaven dad?

Cleophisis: Well baby let's just say it's all that and a bag of funyuns! We had a party last night in the Garden of Eden and Eve was the chaperone. Michael Jackson was moon walking on air after our choir rehearsal and Noah was doing the electric slide with Job.

Sharlice: Wow dad it sounds like fun, I can't wait to join you.

Cleophsis: Sounds like you have some sorting out to do first before you can come up to the pearly blue skies baby girl. I'm going to sit here and watch and I want you to make things right in your house again. You can look to me for strength if you need to. I know you can do it so don't let me down! (Goes in the corner of room and sits down)

Tiny: (Walks in as Sharlice is getting up from her knees) Hey Sharlice we need to talk!

Sharlice: (Mouth is open in shock as Tiny has on new threads and has cut his nappy afro off) Oh Tiny you look so nice.

Tiny: Thanks, you have a minute.

Sharlice: Yes Sir, anything for you Mr. Tiny!

Tiny: I want to apologize for my actions earlier today. I'm sorry and I know you don't deserve to be treated like that. You are my beautiful, beautiful queen and I'm blessed to have such a fine woman of God.

Sharlice: That's okay Tiny. I said some things I shouldn't have said either. I was so busy looking at your faults that I couldn't see all the wonderful qualities that I have in you.

Tiny: I seen this church on TV called Behind The Veil and I would like us to visit. The Pastor, Pastor V is so anointed and speaks the word of God with authority. Maybe she could counsel us too.

Sharlice: I'd love to go and maybe she could even help you with your two step I mean one and a half step (Doing stepping motion).

Tiny: Oh you got jokes! Well you were all up on my two left feet when we met that night at the Soul Train. You had so much Vaseline on your face that I didn't even have to turn on my headlights that night when we left.

Sharlice: Boy you so silly. You know my mama made me do it though!

Evernesia: (Walks in with Unique) Hello newlyweds, how r u doing?

Tiny: Hey mama, can I still call you if I ever nes a

Evernesia: Only if I can see your tiny toonbox turn big

Sharlice: Yall so silly, we fine mama and Unique, we are so sorry you had to be in the middle of our argument earlier today

Unique: That's okay I guess that's what couples do

Tiny: Yeah you got that right! Boy I never seen the righteous forsaken or his seed begging bread and Lord knows we've had our share of bread!

Unique: Next time I'll just quietly remove myself so I won't be forced to choose sides

Sharlice: Good idea baby

Tiny: Hey Sharlice what was that song you were listening too this morning

Sharlice: Oh yall got to hear it, its Marvin Sapp's new song. He's saying when everyone else judges you, God only see's the best in you. When everyone puts you down and talks about you, God only sees the best in you. When everyone brings up your pass and all your faults, God only sees the best in you.

Evernesia: Go head girl, Preach it to us! Turns to the audience how many of yall ready for a word on this side? I can't hear you! How many of yall ready for a word on this side? How bout in the middle?
All right now I need you all to follow me on this one

If you're ready for the word clap your hands
(Pause)
If you're ready ready ready like meatball and spaghetti if you're ready ready ready clap your hands

If you're really, really ready stomp your feet
If really think you're ready lose your seat

Sharlice: Mama you so crazy (Laughing)! I ain't no minister, that's some hard work; I'm just telling it like it is. Now like I was saying that song really blessed my soul.

Tiny: Well stop yapping and make it happen woman! I mean when we gone get to hear it!

Sharlice: Okay, I'll play the song! (Walks over to cut the radio on)

(Everyone circles in the middle of the room for a group hug)

The End

When Purpose Meets Praise

Written by:
Brother Luther T. Collins

Intro

Church Setting where the Pastor has guest preacher at their 1 year anniversary.
The guest Pastor preaches and teaches on ones person being introduced to dynamic praise causing an explosion throughout the church by way of a domino effect.
THIS PLAY IS A SPINOFF OF "WHAT WOULD JESUS DO"

Scene 1

Musician & Drummer: (Begins music) Mmmm, Mmmm, Mmmm; Mmmm, Mmmm, Mmmm; Mmmm, Mmmm, Mmmm

Choir: (Evangelist Kizzi, Sister Shaquanna Showme, and Brother Earlray Aldridge enters in dancing down main aisle on one accord with the drummer and keyboard player already in place as the choir director follows behind with a grand entrance)

(Everyone takes there places as the choir director prompts the beginning of the opening selection by raising and dropping his hands with his director stick in hand)

Choir: "Purpose & Praise"

Minister Innis: (Gives signal to stop music) Let's talk purpose and praise for a minute (Begins chant as the choir goes wild) Give me a P

Choir: You got your P you got your P

Minister Innis: Give me a U

Choir: You got your U you got your U

Minister Innis: Give me a R

Choir: You got your R you got your R

Minister Innis: Give me a P

Choir: You got your P you got your P

Minister Innis: Give me a O

Choir: You got your O you got your O

Minister Innis: Give me a S

Choir: You got your S you got your S

Minister Innis: Give me a E

Choir: You got your E you got your E

Minister Innis: Give me another P

Choir: You got your P you got your P

Minister Innis: Give me a R

Choir: You got your R you got your R

Minister Innis: Give me a A

Choir: You got your A you got your A

Minister Innis: Give me a I

Choir: You got your I you got your I

Minister Innis: Give me a S

Choir: You got your S you got your S

Minister Innis: Give me a E

Choir: You got your E you got your E

Minister Innis: Now what that spell

Choir: "Purpose & Praise"

Minister Tiny Soulville & Brother Neckbone: (Drops the beat) Mmmm, Mmmm, Mmmm, Mmmm, Mmmm, Mmmm, Mmmm, Mmmm, Mmmm, Mmmm, Mmmm, Mmmm, Mmmm

Choir: "Purpose & Praise"

Minister Tiny Soulville & Brother Neckbone: (Drops the beat) Mmmm, Mmmm, Mmmm, Mmmm, Mmmm, Mmmm, Mmmm, Mmmm, Mmmm, Mmmm, Mmmm, Mmmm, Mmmm

Choir: "Purpose & Praise"

Minister Innis: (Signals for the song end and for everyone to take seats by spinning finger around and pointing both index fingers towards the wall)

Pastor Palby: Welcome saints to our 1 year, naw 365 days, naw 52 weeks, naw 26 bi-weeks anniversary here at the Saints of Praise Sanctuary Presbyterian, Baptismal, Episcopal, Cathletic Church. And we still here even when they said we wouldn't make it. We still here after my wife's pot roast burned down the church. We still here after one of the visitors let loose in the baptismal pool. We still here after the FBI served that warrant on Brother Malcolm Fleas for selling drugs in the church. We still here after being evicted twice and having our church van repossessed. So I just wanna know is there a praise in the house?

Choir: Praising low

Pastor Palby: Yall better praise him like yall know up in here. When you was at the club last night you didn't have a problem raising the roof so what's the problem now? I'm talking bout my savior, your savior, the alpha, the omega, the first, the last, do I need to keep on going? Without God our purpose is nonexistent on today or any day.

Minister Innis: (Jumps up in circles shouting) I, I got a praise, I got a praise and I gotta let it out, I gotta praise. I, I got a praise, I got a praise and I gotta let it out, I gotta praise!

Pastor Palby: There go that praise I was looking for! Let go and let God son!

Choir: (Stands together singing) He, he got a praise and he gotta let it out, he gotta praise! (Repeat)

(Musicians play shouting music)

(Minister Innis begins to praise in dance)

Pastor Palby: And let the church say Amen!

Church Responds: Amen

Pastor Palby: Everybody put your hands together as Sister Shaquanna comes up with this morning's announcements.

Sister Shaquanna: Good morning church. Today's announcements are as follows. Today we have our chitlin bake off immediately following service hosted by Deaconess Umba Cotae. Friday will be our children's jam for Jesus and our very own Pastor Palby will be our guest mc. And last but not least this Sunday immediately following evening service we will be having our junk in your trunk yard sale. So empty out your trunks and let's fill the church lawn with all your junk. That concludes this morning's announcements. Let's govern ourselves accordingly!

Pastor Palby: Thank you Sister Shaquanna. Let us welcome my lovely wife Evangelist Kizzi Ramon as she comes up and blesses us with our Church Itty Bitty Committee Acknowledgements.

Evangelist Kizzi: On behalf of our church, what's the name of our church, oh I'm sorry, The Saint's of Praise Sanctuary Presbyterian, Baptismal, Episcopal, Catholic Church, we here at the Itty Bitty Committee would like to first acknowledge our Pastor and my husband for one year of devotion and dedication. It just goes to show you God can use anybody. You would have never known Pastor Palby was in jail for armed robbery just two years ago.

Minister Innis: (Stands up and interrupts the service) Wait, HOLD the communion cup, you mean to tell me my Pastor was in jail for armed robbery. What he rob a bank or something? Will a man rob God? I'm outta here, you won't have me setting it off up in here. (Walking off)

Evangelist Kizzi: What about forgiveness Minister? God forgave him so you can too.

Minister Innis: Oh I forgive him but I definitely won't forget. (Searching his pockets) Man I forgot my bus pass expired I'm a just sit in the back of the church but I got my eyes on you Pastor.

Evangelist Kizzi: On behalf of the Itty Bitty Committee we would like to thank Deacon Little and Deacon Smalls for fixing the roof after the fire. And just for the record church it wasn't pot roast I was cooking it was Baby Chicken Casserole. Deacons come on up and share a few words of wisdom with us.

Deacon Smalls and Deacon Little: Praise the Lord Saints

Deacon Smalls: (Singing) Is there a heart in the house tonight

Minister Innis: (Raises his hands)

Deacon Little: (Singing) Stand up and let you me know you understand

Deacon Smalls: (Singing) You got to have love

Minister Innis: (Begins to sing) A heart is for house of love and I've learned

Minister Tiny Soulville: (Sings back up) I've learned

Minister Innis: (Singing) That it don't take much to break a heart

Minister Tiny Soulville: (Sings back up) You got to build it up

Minister Innis: (Singing) Let me know that you understand

Evangelist Kizzi: (Singing) Ahhewwhewe. (Closes out song)

Deacons: (Go sit down)

Evangelist Kizzi: Man I was feeling that thing all in my soul yall. I just see God doing some extravagant things in this house tonight. That concludes our little teeny tiny itty bitty committee.

Pastor Palby: Thank you Evangelist Kizzi! And thank you for that delicious Baby Bird Tuna Casserole; it was awesome before it burned down the church.

Evangelist Kizzi: (Stands up) That was a "Chicken Bird" casserole I mean baby chicken casserole.

Pastor Palby: Oh I'm sorry baby it was so good that I even ate the feathers. Brother Earlray won't you come on up and welcome our first time visitors.

Brother Earlray: Praise the Lord everybody, I would ask that all visitors stand

Minister Innis: (Stands)

Brother Earlray: Minister Innis this is for the first time visitors

Minister Innis: I'm a born again visitor. If Pastor can take a blood bath so can I.

Brother Earlray: So be it Minister Innis! Brother Neckbone won't you come join me in presenting our gift to the first time visitors

Brother Neckbone: (Comes up) Praise the Lord Brethren (country accent) we got something special lined up for you today that you can't get anywhere else. We gone start off simple with some good ol fashion country line square dancing yee haw!

Brother Earlray: I don't do no country line square dancing Brother Neckbone

Brother Neckbone: Well I guess I'll have to save that for my trial sermon, "Country Soul Food in Heaven". Minister Tiny Soulville drop it on the one!

Minister Tiny Soulville: Like we always do around here

Brother Earlray & Brother: (Sing welcome song)
We wanna welcome you this morning
We wanna welcome you this morning
To the Saints of Praise (Pause) Sanctuary
To the Saints of Praise (Pause) Sanctuary
Presbyterian (Extend and then pause)
Baptismalllllll (Hold and then pause)
Episcopal (Fast)
Cath letic Church
For God is here
And now you are here
So let's join in together
And praise without fear, we said praise without fear
Thank you --------- for coming to our church!

Pastor Palby: Praise the Lord, yall got me ready to join again. Well church it's time for the word. And boy do we have a special treat in store for you today. All the way from Johattausberg, Mars stand up and put your hands together for Minister Sophie.

Minister Sophie: (Makes grand entrance with armor bearer Sister So & So)

Sister So & So: (Carries duffle bag for Minister Sophie and gets her things together i.e. bible)

Minister Sophie: Put yo hands up! Now putem down real fast! When the Lord speaks yall better listen. Put your hands up! Now putem back down real fast! Praise the Lord. I almost didn't make it today because the moving shuttle was late to my house.

Everyone: Shuttle!

Minister Sophie: Yea it's getting to hot in Mars so I've decided to move to Jupiter. We are getting to close to the sun so it's time for me to go. It's so hot in Mars that the moon asked God if he could relocate. I'm so glad to be here today at your one year anniversary. I just got one question, what's the name of yall church again, never mind, I probably won't remember it anyway. Yall need to get it in the phonebook so I call sometimes. I tried to call yall collect but the operator said she never heard of a Presbyterian Baptismal Episcopal Cathletic church. What do yall baptize Cathletics in the sanctuary and the Presbyterians in an Episcopal church? Now that we got that out the way let's get down to business, before I get into my sermon I need know if yall got my shuttle ticket and the itinerary so I can get back home. I left pootsie and wootsie home alone and I don't want them getting no ideas.

Sister So & So: Minister we got all we need, they blessed us with a shuttle ticket, an international food stamp card, and some pot roast to get us back home.

Minister Sophie: Well praise (Hold) the Lord! (Dancing around doing a mini shout)

Musicians: (Began playing praise music)

Pastor Palby: Take your time Minister Sophie! Take your time!

Minister Sophie: Today church we gone talk about Purpose and Praise! First I wanna know if we have any fools in the house and when I say fools I mean fools for Jesus. I mean you'll do anything and say anything that lines up with the word. Not with your own choice words but Gods words. I wanna know will you work it out for God? Will you show off for him? See let me tell you a story: There was this Indian and his son. Well the Indian told his son to go find wood and his son said but why dad. And The Indian said because I'm yo daddy is that a good enough reason and the son said yea dad (With a disappointing sigh). The son came back 15 minutes later with enough wood to build a house. The dad began to do an Indian dance like never before and it rubbed off and his son begins to dance and sing in their native language. After the dance the dad cooked wood stew, wooden stew burgers, and built them a wood teepee that got them thru the winter and they lived happily ever after. The point of this story is when God says do something you don't question him. He's your daddy and you never question what your daddy is doing, you just do it like Nike. Besides where you think they got that slogan from. A father told his son just do it and Nikes were born is my guess. God gives everyone in life a purpose not based on what you want to do but based on what he called you to do. You have to fulfill your calling without complaining but with a can do or praise attitude. Did you know Hell is hot and your perm won't last in the heat? Can you image trying to put on makeup in hell? Well just let me tell you it won't work. Not even your tears can cool you off. See when your purpose meets praise you better look out cause all the angels will party like its 1999. I'm talking tongue talking, praise walking, walls shattering, roaches chattering, ground breaking, and heaven shaking unlike nothing you've ever seen or heard before. So don't be afraid to let your praise power your purpose. If you acted like a fool before you were saved now you really need to act fool, go crazy, lose your mind, get drunk in Jesus, not gin, not juice but don't be afraid to let your spirit loose. Raise the roof in praise and make it rain.

....
....
………….. Minister Sophie will freestyle the rest of sermon (Should be no less than 15 minutes, uses some kind of analogy by pulling people and pulling items out of bag, using scripture of choice, continuing on combining purpose and praise and ending in the results of purpose and praise leading to prayers being answered, pausing frequently during sermon and even asking if anyone has any questions)

Minister Innis: (During question and answer session) Would you follow a Pastor who has a criminal record and is a first time felon?

Minister Sophie: Were you not listening to my sermon! Put yo hands up! Now putem down real fast!

Minister Innis: (Puts hands up and down just as she says)

Minister Sophie: When God speaks you better listen! If God says go than you go!

Minister Innis: What if your Pastor was convicted of armed robbery and lost his right to bear arms?

Minister Sophie: Did the offering plate come up short?

Minister Innis: Yes Ma'am

Minister Sophie: Did your church get evicted or lose power

Minister Innis: We had a lock out and power outage on the same day and our church was chained up.

Minister Sophie: When you prayed what did God say?

Minister Innis: I'm still waiting for an answer

Minister Sophie: Put yo hands up! Now putem down real fast! When God speaks yall better listen! God don't take long if he puts you on hold you may want to check your palm pilot because something may be wrong with your connection! If you can't hear God that means you got too many people texting you! You better remove some of that clutter from your life. It's like having so much wax in your ears that you have to get your ears drained weekly.

Sister So & So: (Puts robe on Minister Sophie when she finishes preaching)

Pastor Palby: (Comes up) Wasn't that awesome yall? What better way to celebrate our first year than to receive such a blessed word from Minister Sophie all the way from another planet to deliver us a powerful word on our 1 year anniversary. Well Minister Sophie if it's not too much trouble we would like for you to come up here and close us out but I do have one special request.

Church: Uhh Ohh!

Pastor Palby: On our opening day here at The Saint's of Praise Sanctuary Presbyterian, Baptismal, Episcopal, Cathletic Church we raised the roof with our theme song and I want us to take it back in celebration of 1 year and we would ask that Minister Sophie and Sister So & So join us as we act a fool for Christ up in here. I want you all to let go and let the spirit move freely throughout this place in celebration. And without any further delay I give you Minister Sophie to close us out.

Minister Sophie: I don't know what song yall talking bout but you know I'm always ready to party for JC! Ain't no party like a Holy Ghost party cause a Holy Ghost party don't stop! I say ain't no party like a Holy Ghost party cause a Holy Ghost party don't stop! Everybody in the whole house (pause) Put yo hands up real fast! Now putem down! When God speaks yall better listen. Put yo hands up! Now putem down real fast! I said real fast now hurry up! Put yo hands up real fast! Now putem down real fast! God please save the lost in here and use them for your purpose and not their own agenda. Please let your grace and mercy not run out while they walk on the red carpet. Give them your features and not their own because Lord some of these features just ain't working for them. Blessem Lord. Let them save themselves before it's too late by voluntarily confessing with their tongue that you are Lord. Let them not get caught in the rapture. May the sweet communion of the Holy Spirit rest rule and abide within us all. And let the church say Amen, say Amen, and Boom Shockalocka!

Pastor Palby: Now everyone in the house stand to your feet as we lose our minds in God introducing our praise to Gods purpose in our life with our theme song!
(The Presence of The Lord starts by Byron Cage and everyone dances and goes crazy)!

The End

78

Don't Change The Station

Written By:

Brother Luther T. Collins

Intro

Pastor Palby and Minister Innis get an invite to come to the radio station. Minister Innis goes on the radio solo until they get wind that Pastor Palby is waiting in the car. During their visit they do not hold back but have a Holy Ghost good time while live on the radio.

Scene 1

DJ Matthew, Mark, Luke & John: Christ Fm 7 3 8 where Jesus is Lord and the gospel is shared around the world

(Plays music) Sweet, beautiful, soul saving joy oh joy, joy down in my soul
The lily of the valley

(Music mix drop)

(Music dies out)

DJ Eve, Esther, Mary, & Ruth: Christ Fm 7 3 8 where Jesus is Lord and the gospel is shared around the world

Dj Matthew, Mark, Luke, & John: What's up, What's up, What's up Detroit?

Dj Eve, Esther, Mary & Ruth: Boy how many times I got to tell you, you ain't Martin, and we ain't in Detroit no more. That was last week!

Dj Matthew, Mark, Luke, & John: Oh that's right we repping Richmond, V A here at Behind the Veil under the fresh anointing of Pastor V. I'm DJ Matthew, Mark, Luke, & John and she's Dj Eve, Esther, Mary, & Ruth live from the world's hottest gospel station in the nation Christ Fm 7 3 8 where Jesus is Lord and the gospel is shared around the world!

Dj Eve, Esther, Mary, & Ruth: Today yall we have a special treat in store for you! We have a very special guest stopping by today guaranteed to bless your spirits.

Dj Matthew, Mark, Luke, & John: Is it Fred Hammond

Dj Eve, Esther, Mary, & Ruth: No silly

Dj Matthew, Mark, Luke, & John: Kelonte Gavin

Dj Eve, Esther, Mary & Ruth: No silly

Dj Matthew, Mark, Luke, & John: Prophetess Juanita Bynum

Dj Eve, Esther, Mary, & Ruth: No silly

Dj Matthew, Mark, Luke, & John: Bishop TD Jakes

Dj Eve, Esther, Mary, & Ruth: No silly

Dj Matthew, Mark, Luke, & John: Pastor James T. Elam Jr.

Dj Eve, Esther, Mary, & Ruth: No silly

Dj Matthew, Mark, Luke, & John: Bishop Darren L. Gay Sr.

Dj Eve, Esther, Mary, & Ruth: No silly

Dj Matthew, Mark, Luke, & John: The Clark Sisters

Dj Eve, Esther, Mary, & Ruth: No silly

Dj Matthew, Mark, Luke, & John: Apostle Travis Jennings

Dj Eve, Esther, Mary, & Ruth: You'll never guess so you might as well stop wasting your breath! It's actually one of your rivals from back in the day.

Dj Matthew, Mark, Luke, & John: I don't know if I like this yall.

Dj Eve, Esther, Mary, & Ruth: Walk in love DJ Matthew, Mark, Luke, & Johnny. Luke 6:27 says love your enemies as you love yourself, bless those who curse, do good to those that mistreat you, if someone slaps you offer them the other cheek with gladness

Dj Matthew, Mark, Luke, & John: Hold on now DJ Eve, Esther, Mary, & Ruthann let me just stop you there. I'm saved sanctified and full of the Holy Ghost but if you hit me than I'm hit you back. You better believe that. I've been known to black out quite frequently and conveniently during times of adversity. As a matter of fact I still couldn't tell you to this day what happened when I got into that fight with Cain and Abel. You woulda thought they would have put up a better fight being brothers and all but Noah gave me more of a run for my money fighting at 826 years of age. Throwing his walker at me and hitting me in the head with his cane talking bout he loves me with the love of the lord.

Dj Eve, Esther, Mary, & Ruth: Boy you so crazy. Right now we would like to introduce our guest for today as he enters into the studio. So let's give a warm welcome for Minister Alfeterze Turrae Cleoophis Annestezia Elephante Innis!

Minister Innis: Praise the Lord's saints! It's good to be here!

Dj Eve, Esther, Mary, & Ruth: It's good to have you here Minister Innis. So tell us a little about yourself. Where did you grow up? What do you do? And where do you draw your inspiration from?

Minister Innis: I grew up in the Boogie Down Bronx with Biggie Smalls and Too Pops

Dj Matthew, Mark, Luke, & John: It's all good baby baby but I thought you grew up here in Richmond, VA

Minister Innis: Ohh I'm sorry, my bag I grew up in Creighton Court something like the Bronx where you have to protect your neck but I tend to confuse it with the Boogie Down sometimes.

Dj Matthew, Mark, Luke, & John: Wow the streets was that tough hugh?

Minister Innis: Naw but my momma was! I'll never forget the day she jacked my sister up against the locker in middle school in front of everybody.

Dj Eve, Esther, Mary, & Ruth: So tell everyone out there in radio land what is it that you do?

Minister Innis: That's a good question because I don't even know what I do. Sometimes I think I'm a song writer. Sometimes I think I'm a singer. Sometimes I think I'm a dancer but if I had to sum it all up I would just go with a sosida musician in the spiritual realm.

Dj Matthew, Mark, Luke, & John: So you do a little dancing hugh?

Minister Innis: Yeah I reckon! We was suppose to be on American's best dance crew last year but Pastor Palby Latté Ramón broke his neck break dancing at altar call.

Dj Matthew, Mark, Luke, & John: Great day! Not break dancing with two left feet!

Dj Eve, Esther, Mary, & Ruth: Why was he break dancing at altar call?

Minister Innis: One of the elders of the church challenged him to a dance off in an effort to raise our soul saver thermometer.

Dj Matthew, Mark, Luke, & John: Wow yall really know how to church over there. What's the name of your church again?

Minister Innis: The Saints of the Sanctuary Presbyterian Baptismal Episcopal Cathletic Church

Dj Eve, Esther, Mary, & Ruth: Well Minister Innis we'll be going to our break shortly but before we do we would like to take some calls. But before we take some calls I just got to know what's up with the choir robe?

Minister Innis: Oh you ain't heard we won the gospel choir contest hosted by Bobby Brown oops I meant Bobby Jones 1 month ago and I haven't took it off since.

Dj Matthew, Mark, Luke, & John and Dj Eve, Esther, Mary & Ruth: (Slide their chairs over quietly away from Minister Innis)

Dj Matthew, Mark, Luke, & John: On that note let's go to the call line

Dj Eve, Esther, Mary, & Ruth: Caller you're on the air

Caller 1: Yes this message is for Minister Innis, Why did you become a Minister and how did you know it was your time?

Minister Innis: Well you know I never wanted to be minister. I didn't choose this, God chose me and when God places a call on your life you can't run from it, trust me I know. My running led me to the water where I ended up in the same whale as Jonah.

Dj Eve, Esther, Mary, & Ruth: He's so right caller, when God puts a calling on your life you can run but you definitely can't hide from God.

Dj Eve, Esther, Mary, & Ruth: Caller 2 you're on the air.

Caller 2: Minister Innis when is the next tour

Minister Innis: At the end of this segment I'll be touring in the parking lot with the Jam Pony Express. I got bootleg CD's and DVD's that I sell out of my car. And I tour every Sunday at the The Saints of the Sanctuary Presbyterian Baptismal Episcopal Cathletic Church located at 2100 I don't wanna go to hell because it's too HOT street drive crescent place circle

Dj Eve, Esther, Mary, & Ruth: Let's take one more call and then we have to go to break, caller 3 you're on the air

Caller 3: I'm a musician at heart what advice can you give me Minister Innis

Minister Innis: Go to school, eat your wheaties, and brush your teeth everyday because ain't nothing worse than a musician with stank breath, but most importantly pray and seek God's face

Dj Eve, Esther, Mary, & Ruth: Minister Innis you are something else! Next time you come out you definitely have to bring your choir and Pastor.

Minister Innis: Oh they here, they out in the car!

Dj Eve, Esther, Mary, & Ruth: In the car, why didn't you bring them in?

Minister Innis: Cause yall ain't ask me too and we had a hard time getting 9 people in Pastors 1993 Sky Blue Ford Escort Station Wagon. Since the church van was repoed we had to take Pastors car.

DJ: Eve, Esther, Mary, & Ruth: I thought your Pastor drove a Benz Coup Deville

Minister Innis: In his mind it is but NO MAAM in reality it's a 1993 Sky Blue Ford Escort Station Wagon

Dj Eve, Esther, Mary, & Ruth: (Laughing out of control) Go get them silly

Dj Matthew, Mark, Luke, & John: Now you know I ain't ready for Pastor Palby Latté Ramón just yet

Minister Innis: Oh that's right he smacked your mama in the face for not pleading the blood on consecration Sunday at altar call and you didn't do anything about it

Dj Matthew, Mark, Luke, & John: It's called agape Minister Innis, you should try it sometimes

Minister Innis: My faith ain't made it that far yet! I'm scared I may black out and just loose it in the Holy Ghost.

Dj Matthew, Mark, Luke, & John: We'll on that note we gone go to break yall. Pastor Palby Latte Ramon will be filling in for me after the break as we turn you over to the wheels of steel!

End of Scene 1

Scene 2

DJ Matthew, Mark, Luke, & John: Christ Fm 7 3 8 where Jesus is Lord and the gospel is shared around the world

(Plays music) Sweet, beautiful, soul saving joy oh joy, joy down in my soul
The lily of the valley

(Music mix drop)

(Music dies out)

(Minister Innis and Dj Eve, Esther, Mary, & Ruth prepare to go back on the air)

(Pastor Palby Latte Ramon enters the studio)

Dj Eve, Esther, Mary, & Ruth: Well we back yall! Let us give a warm welcome to Pastor Palby Latté Ramón and his Armor Bearer Brother Malcolm Fleas.

Pastor Palby: (Hollering in the microphone) Praise the Lord Saints, For this is the day the Lord has made and I shall rejoice and be glad in it (Pastor poots out loud)

Brother Malcolm Fleas: Excuse him Dj Eve, Esther, Mary, & Ruth he can't help it! It's in his blood!

Dj Eve, Esther, Mary, & Ruth: (Holds her breath and slides away from Pastor Palby) So Pastor Palby what yall doing sitting out in the car and is there anyone else outside?

Pastor Palby: (Looking over at Minister Innis) Well Dj Eve, Esther, Mary, & Ruth Minister Innis told us he was running in to do a quick song and he would be right back

Minister Innis: Did I say song I meant I was running in real quick and it shouldn't be too long

Brother Malcolm Fleas: Is that right (Looking at Minister Innis real hard like)

Minister Innis: Yes that's right Minister Elect Malcolm Fleas

Dj Eve, Esther, Mary, & Ruth: So Brother Malcolm Fleas is now Minister Elect, how did this come to be

Minister Innis: Well let's see we had a vote and it just so happened that he won by a landslide

Dj Eve, Esther, Mary, & Ruth: Yall had a vote, Pastor Palby what's up with that

Pastor Palby: Well Sister since we are a baptismal church we have to vote for everything

Dj Eve, Esther, Mary, & Ruth: So does that mean that you could be voted out at any time

Pastor Palby: Naw cause then I wouldn't be able to pay my child support. If they vote me out I'm filing for unemployment!

Dj Eve, Esther, Mary, & Ruth: All right yall we running a little behind. Minister Innis would you mind telling your audience your local upcoming church events in place of DJ Matthew, Mark, Luke, & John

Minister Innis: Ola Ola Ola, Ola Ola Ola

Bro Malcolm & Pastor Palby: Ola Ola Ola, Ola Ola Ola

Minister Innis: Ohle Ohle Ohle let me tell you now!

Bro Malcolm & Pastor Palby: Ohle Ohle Ohle let me tell you now!

Minister Innis: At the conclusion of the Sunday's service we will be having chitlens, egg foo young, sweet peter jeter, and poppy seeds in the basement immediately after service! Next Saturday we are having a soul saving surprise marathon at Pastor V's house

Bro Malcolm Fleas: Does Pastor V know about this surprise marathon?

Minister Innis: No fool that's why I said surprise. I just hope she's not listening to the radio

Pastor Palby: We are guests in her church and I think she's in the audience

Minister Innis: We'll I guess it isn't gone be no surprise, surprise, surprise

Bro Malcolm: Naw Gomer Pyle we ain't doing this not in this radio station

Pastor Palby: Be sure to join us Wednesday night for an hour of power at our jam for Jesus pot roast casualty with our hostess with the mostest Sister Umba Cotae

Bro Malcolm: Right on

Minister Innis: And last but not least join us this Tuesday for Pastor Palby's homegoing service

Bro Malcolm: Where you going

Pastor Palby: I'm going up in yonder

Everyone: He's going up in yonder

Pastor Palby: To be with my lord

Bro Malcolm: But why

Pastor Palby: Cause I can't take the pain, salvations not a game

Minister Innis: He forgot he can't sang

Brother Malcolm: I know it's just a shame

Pastor Palby: I used to sang in Spain

Minister Innis: Hell is not a game

Dj Eve, Esther, Mary, & Ruth: Yall funny! It's time to pay some bills as we have another special guest coming to the show

Guest 1: Little Suzy from Charlottesville come on in

Dj Eve, Esther, Mary, & Ruth: Let us welcome you Little Suzy, tell us a little about yourself, how old are you and what school do you go to

Guest 1: I'm 11 years old and I go to school at the Living Saints School of Arts

Dj Eve, Esther, Mary, & Ruth: When did you first get saved?

Guest 1: At the age of 7

Dj Eve, Esther, Mary, & Ruth: Why did you feel it was important to get saved and give your life to God at even a young age?

Guest 1: I wanted to be different and I don't like it when it gets too hot so salvation sounded like a great investment to me

Dj Eve, Esther, Mary, & Ruth: Does everyone support you in your decision

Guest 1: My Uncle Clarentine was not too fond of my decision but what does he know he's still stuck in 60's after all this time

Dj Eve, Esther, Mary & Ruth: And are you able to spread the word with your friends

Guest 1: Yes, I'm not ashame of the gospel

Dj Eve, Esther, Mary, & Ruth: Praise the lord, that's what it's all about saving souls

Minister Innis: I second that motion

Pastor Palby: I third that motion

Bro Malcolm Fleas: I fourth that motion

Dj Eve, Esther, Mary, & Ruth: Thank you all for joining us here today on Christ FM 7 3 8 where Jesus is Lord and the gospel is shared with the world. We give a warm welcome to our guests today Minister Innis, Pastor Palby Latté Ramón, Minister Elect Malcolm Fleas & Little Ms Sister Suzy! We down to our last 10 minutes of the show as we go into our blast off starting with reflections by Minister Elect Malcolm Fleas

Minister Elect Malcolm Fleas:
Don't let me scare you, Just let me tell you about his love and his grace,
For he died for you and me so put a smile on your face,
Rose from the dead on the third day,
Nailed to the cross just so your sins could go away,
Can you image the pain, the suffering, and everything he went through?
But we get a bad report and throw in the towel just because it's all about you,
Wake up smell the funk,
Open your eyes and put the faith in the trunk,
Remove all the junk
And fill up in love only based on what is real,
The living word of God I'm talking not what you feel,
See deception & defeat but don't receive it,
Accept what's in the word & believe it,
Only acknowledge the true sovereign God before it's too late,
If you play with fire you get burnt so I won't participate,
Don't be killed in the fire,

But walk on the water and kill your flesh along with your desire,
Line up to the word and feed your spirit,
After confessing share with your friends so the world can hear!
May your fart not stink (Looking over at Pastor Palby) and your breath be still!
Time is of the essence for only God can reveal!

Dj Eve, Esther, Mary, & Ruth: All right, there you have it from our very own Minister Elect Malcolm Fleas! Well I hope you enjoyed our show today. These mighty men of God have really blessed us on today! Join us next week as we set sail to the Bahamas in a mission to save lost souls! And we don't just want to leave you high and dry but we have something special from our very own Pastor Palby Latté Ramón!

Pastor Palby: Bless you all for coming to our show, thank you for your love but now we got to go, now drop that beat!
(Pastor Palby performs gospel hip hop)

The End

Together We Stand

Written by:

Luther T. Collins

Introduction

A newly wedded couple of 1 year is still adjusting to life with a blended family. The kids are struggling to get along as they are at each other's throat every other day. The husband and wife are standing on love and prayer to get them through the tough times but will it be enough? The ex-wife slithers her way back into the picture after being released from jail. Big mama finds herself playing mediator and equalizer during dysfunctional times.

Characters

Leroy Potter – father

Margie Lareisha Potter – mother

Shelby Hennessey Lareisha – Margie's daughter

Junior Potter – Leroy's son

Summer Alize Lareisha – Shelia's daughter

Big Mama – Leroy's Mom

Aretha Potter – Leroy's Ex-wife

Scene 1

Leroy: (Playing hiding go seek with Summer as they are walking towards the house, pops out and grabs her by surprise as she comes around the corner) Gotcha dumplin

Summer: (Laughing) Oh Daddy

Margie: Yall are having too much fun, sometimes I think you married me for my baby

Leroy: I did, not the big one though

Margie: Now you know Shelby ain't that bad

Leroy: In what world

Margie: Well what about Junior, he ain't no saint you know. I would swear he was raised by wolves

Leroy: Hey watch yourself, I did the best I could with what I had

Margie: That's the sad part, who names their son Junior anyway? Junior is meant to be a continuation of the bloodline. Otherwise we just got a Junior Walker Junior.

Leroy: You need to be thanking me from saving you from being a life-long Lareisha; you got to come to the Potters house and didn't have to pay a thing

Margie: Whatever, don't let me get started on that ex wife of yours, that woman of God watched set it off and thought she was gone Set It Off at If God Be For You Christian Credit Union, all the way from the pulpit to the prison cell. And to take her armor bearers with her to rob a bank, she didn't hear from God that day. Will a sister rob God, I guess so!

Leroy: Don't say nothing else to me

(Lights dim on them and switch over to the stage/inside the house)

Junior: (Comes out of his room walks in front of the TV on his way to the fridge goes in the fridge and drinks straight out of the container)

Shelby: Did you really just put your dirty, nasty, filthy lips on the container of kool-aid that I just made?

Junior: Yep (burps), Preciate you

Shelby: You trifling

Junior: Yo mama

Shelby: (Walks up to him with a bat in hand) Junior, don't you be talking bout my mama you know I don't play that, I will buss you upside your head

Junior: I'd like to see you try, You forget you in my house, know yo place, get yo hood hopping self up out of my face. Betta play by house rules or else

(Leroy, Margie, & Summer walks in house)

Leroy: What in the sam sausage head is going on in here?

Margie: Summer go in the room with big mama sweetie

Shelby: Yo son bout to get his head knocked slam off

(Margie walks over and snatches bat from Shelby)

Junior: That's right Marg get yo tiger cub under control

(Margie gives Shelby the bat back)

Margie: Know you knock all the hell out of him. I will not be disrespected in my own house by you or anyone else.

(Leroy walks in the middle of them attempting to separate everyone)

Leroy: Now just hold on a Holy Ghost minute, this is not what we do in this house. Now Junior you owe Margie an apology, and don't you ever disrespect my wife like that again.

Junior: Sorry Marg

(Leroy pops him in the back of the head)

Leroy: You got one more time to call her by her first name

Junior: But dad I'm practically grown, I'll be 18 in a month

Leroy: Practically don't pay no bills and you ain't grown until you get out of my house. Do you know what grown stands for Leroy?

Junior: No Sir

Leroy: That's what I thought, grown stands for **Getting Ready for Outside World Now!** And how do you get ready, by moving out. Now apologize or get out of my house.

Junior: Sorry Mrs. Margie

Shelby: What about me?

Junior: What about you?

Shelby: You owe me an apology too

Junior: For what

Shelby: For putting yo nasty, dirty, filthy, stanky lips on the kool aid container

(Leroy walks up to Junior and looks him dead in the eyeballs)

Junior: Sorry Shelby

Leroy: Now listen I know this transition ain't been easy but a family that prays together stays together. Now bow yo heads and hold hands

(Leroy begins praying and gets interrupted in the middle of prayer)

Aretha: (Opens door with key) Would you look at here? My key still works!

(Prayer stops as Leroy, Shelby, Shelia, and Junior all stand amazed)

End of Scene 1

Scene 2

Cliff Hanger

To be Continued in Productions Made Personal Volume II! Be sure to tune in same station (PMP) same story (Together We Stand) to find out what happens next………………………

God Given – God Inspired

www.ingramcontent.com/pod-product-compliance
Lightning Source LLC
Chambersburg PA
CBHW070118110526
44587CB00015BA/2347